THIS BOOK IS FOR MY SON.

—DJC

Copyright © 2021, 2024 by Sourcebooks
Text by Daniel J. Crawford
Cover and internal design © 2024 by Sourcebooks
Cover design by Maryn Arreguín/Sourcebooks
Internal design by Maryn Arreguín and Jessica Nordskog/Sourcebooks

Sourcebooks and the colophon are registered trademarks of Sourcebooks.

All rights reserved.

This publication is designed to provide accurate and authoritative information in regard to the subject matter covered. It is sold with the understanding that the publisher is not engaged in rendering legal, accounting, or other professional service. If legal advice or other expert assistance is required, the services of a competent professional person should be sought.
—From a Declaration of Principles Jointly Adopted by a Committee of the American Bar Association and a Committee of Publishers and Associations

All brand names and product names used in this book are trademarks, registered trademarks, or trade names of their respective holders. Sourcebooks is not associated with any product or vendor in this book.

Published by duopress, an imprint of Sourcebooks
P.O. Box 4410, Naperville, Illinois 60567-4410
(630) 961-3900
sourcebooks.com

Originally published as *Stop Asking "How Was Your Day?": 444 Better Questions to Help You Connect with Your Child* in 2021 in the United States of America by duopress.

Cataloging-in-Publication Data is on file with the Library of Congress.

Printed and bound in China.
OGP 10 9 8 7 6 5 4 3 2 1

STOP ASKING "HOW WAS YOUR DAY?"

444 BET
QUESTIONS TO
CONNECT
YOUR C

duopress
an imprint of sourcebooks

DANIEL J.

WELCOME

This book is a tool. It is an introduction to a conversation.

It began as a list of questions taped to the center console of my beat-up 2000 Toyota, a series of curious conversation starters to help my son, his mother, and myself engage in meaningful after-school discussion. He was five years old when I started writing this list, and we had already fallen into an after-school routine that was incomplete and unproductive. There was (and continues to be) a universe of life expanding in the mind and soul of my child, a universe I care about deeply, but at the end of an exhausting day at school, summarizing the entirety of his day in a single moment became a chore.

Something was missing. I recalled the many times in my own life when I had to sum up an experience on the spot, and I remembered just how challenging that can be.

So, I prepared a list of questions in advance.

Over time, I added more, and the list grew longer. I wrote much of this content as a solution for my own family. But the book you have in front of you, I wrote for you, for the parents and caregivers who love their children very much but are struggling to communicate.

How was school?

How was school?

Did you learn anything today?

How was school?

I was asking my son to reduce six hours of his day into a single-syllable reply. And then we would move on. I was reading the headlines but missing the news.

It wasn't his fault. It was mine.

I was asking the wrong questions.

This book helps to find the right ones. Each page presents questions that, in the moment, we don't think to ask. Some of the questions are fun, some are deep and reflective, and some are silly. Some questions will open doors to otherwise difficult conversations about mental health, personality, and identity. Some questions will encourage you to share things you don't otherwise know how to say. The questions are diverse and are appropriate for schoolchildren of all ages and walks of life. They can be asked in any particular order and can be adjusted toward the individual. In addition, this book offers various "Lead by Example" sections—prompts that will encourage you to share with your child something from your own experience.

Human beings crave communication and connection, but we often struggle to find it. These questions bridge that gap.

It is not necessarily the content of the questions that matters, nor the substance of the replies they elicit. Rather, it is the simple act of communication that carries the greatest weight. Children of all ages will grow to desire some degree of privacy and individuality, and those desires should be respected, of course. This book is not designed as a tool to learn every detail about your child's day. Instead, it is designed to get to know your child as a person, as an individual.

Ultimately, this book is about communication and nothing more. It is comprehensive but demands little time and effort from the parent or caregiver.

In this book, I offer no lectures on parenting. I offer no expertise, no study guides, no lifestyle coaching. I offer only the means to get the ball rolling, to encourage openness, connection, and communication. This book is a tool, to be flipped through while parked in the pickup line at school, before sitting down to dinner, or anywhere and anytime you please.

Communication is valuable in any relationship, but amid day-to-day stresses and exhausting schedules, it can become a challenge. This book provides solutions. You'll find that these questions lead to more in-depth conversations and stronger relationships. I know there is value in this book, as I have already found it. I encourage you to find it too.

Enjoy.

–DANIEL J. CRAWFORD

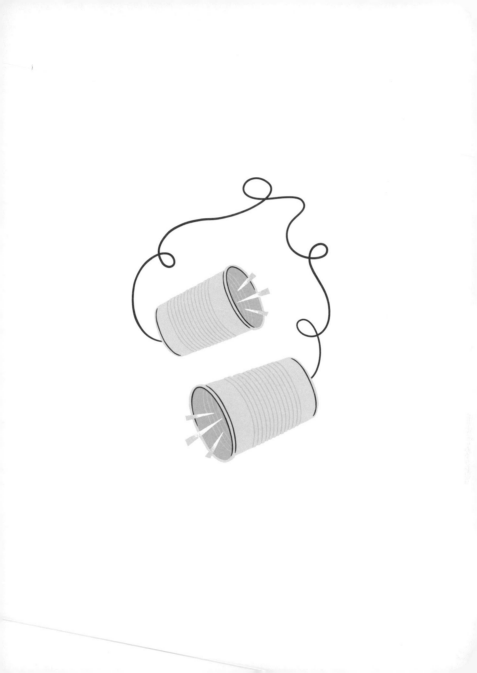

1 **Who sat next to you** at **lunch** today?

 2 If you were a **journalist**, what **news topic** would you want to cover?

3 How do you feel when you **meet someone new?** Are you **outgoing** or **reserved?** Do you feel **confident? Cautious?**

 4 Is there anyone who **tries really hard** but doesn't do well in school?

5 Who is the **most organized** student?

 6 Do you ever have **trouble concentrating?**

 7 Do you think people **act differently** at different times of the day?

 8 Have any of your classmates ever asked **a question that your teacher couldn't answer?**

9 Would you rather travel to school on a **horse** or in a **hot-air balloon**?

10 If we switched places for a week, **how would I do in your classes**? How would you do at **my job**?

11 If you were a phone, how much **battery power** would you have right now?

12 Do you think **everything will turn out okay** this year?

LEAD by EXAMPLE

- IF I COULD GO BACK TO SCHOOL, I WOULD STUDY...

- IF I COULD GIVE ADVICE TO MYSELF AT YOUR AGE, I WOULD SAY...

- THE MOST INQUISITIVE PERSON I KNOW IS...

13 How many **pencils** are in your school?

14 What was **the funniest thing** that happened today?

15 Which **subjects** do you wish they taught in school?

16 What's **one song** you wish you could learn to play on any **instrument**?

LEAD by EXAMPLE

- I'M THANKFUL TO MY PAST SELF FOR...

- A GIFT I AM GIVING TO MY FUTURE SELF IS...

- I FORGIVE MYSELF FOR...

- I AM BLESSED BECAUSE...

17 Do you notice people's **eye color**? What about **hair color** or **skin color**?

18 What's the **oldest memory** that you have?

19 If a **famous chef** came to make lunch for your school, what would all the students **want to eat**?

20 Can you think of a time when you were kind to yourself? Were you **kind to yourself** today?

21 Could you make it through an entire day of being **completely silent**?

22 Could **everyone** in your school go an **entire day** without **speaking**?

23 What makes you **angry** at school?

24 **When you get angry,** how long does it last and what helps you **feel better**?

25 Do you ever wait until **the last minute** to finish something?

 26 Do you think most **punishments** and **rewards** are effective? If you had to choose your own, what would you choose?

 27 Is there anyone you **see** every day but have never **spoken** to?

28 Which **teachers** absolutely **love what they do**?

LEAD by EXAMPLE

- ONE PERSON I REALLY ADMIRED AS A CHILD WAS...

- ONE PERSON I LOOK UP TO NOW IS...

- WHEN I WAS A KID, ONE PERSON WHO HAD A BIG IMPACT ON ME WAS...

29 Why do you think school buses are yellow? **What color would you like your school bus to be?**

 30 What **catchphrase** is everyone **saying** right now?

31 What is a catchphrase I say that someone **your age** would **never say?**

 32 **Who inspires you** to be better?

33 Do you know that **it's okay if you're not perfect?**

34 What's one thing **teachers love** but **students hate?**

35 Do you have **high self-esteem** or **low self-esteem** most of the time?

36 What's **the most fun you've had** in school?

37 What do you think the **principal** does all day?

---

38 Do you like **being in class** when it's **raining** outside? What about when it's **sunny**?

---

39 What is **one thing at school** you are **thankful** for?

---

40 If you could turn your school into a **mini-golf course**, what **obstacles** would you create and how would you **design** it?

LEAD by EXAMPLE

- MY FAVORITE THING ABOUT WHERE WE LIVE IS...

- MY FAVORITE VACATION WE'VE BEEN ON IS...

- ONE PLACE I'VE ALWAYS WANTED TO VISIT IS...

- A COUNTRY I'VE ALWAYS BEEN FASCINATED
  BY IS...

41 If you could **rearrange the alphabet,** what order would you put the letters in?

 42 Do you think **school is harder for you** than it was **for me** at your age?

 43 Do you ever feel like you have to **please everyone**?

44 Would you **learn differently** if you lived in a completely **different country**?

45 Are there any students who **used to be friends** but aren't friends anymore?

46 What's **the longest word** you know?

47 Do you like to **work alone**, with **one other person**, or with **a group**?

48 If you could **redesign our town or city**, what would you add? What would you take away?

49 If you were **in charge of the class,** how would you **settle an argument** between two students?

 50 How many **words** do **you know?**

 51 What is one thing that **other students** are **interested in** that **you aren't?**

52 What is one thing **you're interested in** that **other students aren't?**

LEAD by EXAMPLE

- WHEN I WAS YOUR AGE, MY FAVORITE
  SONG WAS...

- MY FAVORITE BAND WAS...

- THE BEST CONCERT I'VE EVER BEEN TO WAS...

- ONE BAND OR MUSICIAN THAT I'D LIKE TO SEE
  IN CONCERT IS...

53 How much **math** do you think I use on a **daily basis?**

54 What's something **you can teach me** that I don't know?

55 If you started a **charity**, whom or what would you **help?**

56 Did you hear **a new song** that you like this week?

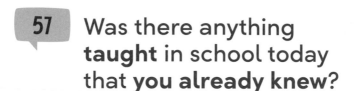

57 Was there anything **taught** in school today that **you already knew?**

58 Are you **afraid** of anything?

59 Does anyone at school **chew on their fingernails** or have any other **nervous habits?**

60 What is your **favorite piece** of **art** that you have ever **created?**

61 When do you feel most **productive**?

62 Is there anyone you have met whom **you didn't like at first** but **grew to like** over time?

63 Do you prefer reading **fiction** or **nonfiction**?

64 Has anyone in school discussed how to **manage your time** and **energy**?

LEAD by EXAMPLE

- I WANT TO BE REMEMBERED FOR...

- I WANT PEOPLE TO ADMIRE ME FOR...

- SOMETHING I'M WORKING ON IS...

- ONE THING I REALLY MISS IS...

- MY LONG-TERM GOALS ARE...

 **65** Is anyone always **drawing** or **doodling** during class?

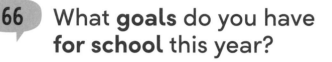 **66** What **goals** do you have **for school** this year?

 67 Have you set any **personal goals** recently? How do you decide what you want to accomplish?

 68 What is one time you **succeeded** in **accomplishing a goal**? What is one time you **failed** to accomplish a goal?

69 What was your **least favorite part** of the day today?

70 Do your teachers seem to **enjoy what they do?**

71 Which **club** or **team** always seems to be **having the most fun?**

 72 What's something **you noticed** today that **no one else noticed?**

What's one thing about **your school** that's **unique**?

 Do you like to **speak or read to the class**?

75 Do you like to **answer questions** when the **teacher asks** the class?

76 Do you ever have trouble **finding joy** in things?

LEAD by EXAMPLE

- I AM MOST RELAXED WHEN...

- I LEARNED WHO I REALLY AM AS A
  PERSON WHEN...

- I THINK ONE OF MY BEST QUALITIES IS...

- TODAY, I WOKE UP THINKING ABOUT...

- A CHALLENGE I FACED AT WORK WAS...

- ONE THING I'M GRATEFUL FOR TODAY IS...

- WHEN I GOT HOME, THE FIRST THING I WANTED
  TO DO WAS...

- TOMORROW, I'M GOING TO PRIORITIZE...

77 Do you **drink water** during the school day?

78 What's your **favorite thing to drink** at school **besides water?**

79 What is one thing that **surprised you** today?

80 Do you feel **at home** within yourself?

81 Who **walks the fastest** in your school?

 82 Who is really **emotionally intelligent**?

 83 Do you prefer learning about **your own country** or **the rest of the world**?

 84 Did any of your **teachers** go to your **school** when they were **younger**?

85 **Who** is in your **friend group?**

---

 86 What do you **like most about your friends?**

---

 87 Is there **anything you don't like** about your **friends?**

---

88 Is there **anyone** who seems to be going through a **hard time** right now?

LEAD by EXAMPLE

- THE BEST JOB I EVER HAD WAS...

- THE HARDEST JOB I EVER HAD WAS...

- MY FIRST JOB WAS...

- ONE JOB I'VE ALWAYS WANTED TO TRY IS...

- THE BEST BOSS I EVER HAD WAS...

- MY FAVORITE COWORKER IS...

- ONE THING I LEARNED IN SCHOOL THAT I USE ALL THE TIME IS...

89 Would you rather take a class on **how to cook meals** or on **how to bake desserts**?

90 How can you tell if a **poem** is good?

91 If a **newspaper** were published about your life, what would **today's headline** be?

92 What kind of **jobs** do you think **other kids** will have when they **finish school**?

93 How does your class **celebrate birthdays?**

 94 What would be **your ideal birthday gift?**

 95 Do you have **friends** who **bring their lunch** to school? Does anyone come with **food that you wish you could try?**

 96 What could you do to **make school better** for students in the future?

97 What is your favorite **smell?**

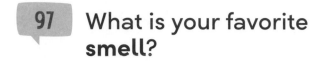 **98** What are you **most proud of** this week?

 99 How many **doors** does your **school** have?

 **100** If your school had a **parade**, what type of **float** would you **create?**

LEAD by EXAMPLE

- WHEN I WAS A KID, I WOULD ALWAYS ASK TO HEAR A STORY ABOUT...

- WHEN I WAS A KID, I LOVED TO READ...

- ONE OF MY FAVORITE BOOKS THAT I'VE READ IS...

- THE LAST BOOK I READ WAS...

- AN ARTICLE I READ THIS WEEK WAS...

101 Do any of your **teachers** have **children**?

102 If you could bring **one musician** to your school to play a **concert**, whom would you ask?

103 Do you think **students 1,000 years ago** felt the same way about education that you do?

104 What makes a **book** really **fun to read**?

105 Which **class** is **the most fun?**

106 Do you **trust people** right when you meet them or do you have to get to know them first?

107 Is it hard or easy to **earn your trust?**

108 What **movies** do kids like to **quote?**

109 Is there anyone who **always talks** but **doesn't listen?**

110 Who has the **loudest voice** in school?

111 Do you have **a strong sense of identity?**

112 Does your **school** do a good job of helping students **discover who they are?**

LEAD by EXAMPLE

- GROWING UP, MY CHORES WERE...

- ONE TIME, I GOT IN A LOT OF TROUBLE FOR...

- ONE TIME, I WAS REWARDED FOR...

113 What **time of day** do you feel your **best**?

114 What's one **brave thing** you've done recently?

115 What **period of history** would you **travel** to if you could?

116 Do you think students are more **motivated** by **rewards** or **punishments**?

117 What are the **most comfortable clothes** you own?

 118 What kind of **math** are you **best** at?

 119 Do you ever have **conversations** with other people **in your head** after the conversation has **already happened**?

 120 Is there **anyone** at school you would like to **get to know better**?

121 Which **teacher** or **staff** member has **the hardest job**?

122 Should there be more education about **money** and **finances**?

123 Are there any **twins** in school? Do they look alike or different?

124 Has someone ever **given their word** and then gone back on it?

LEAD by EXAMPLE

- THE BIGGEST CHALLENGE I HAD TODAY WAS...

- THE BEST DECISION I MADE THIS WEEK WAS...

- A BIG DECISION I NEED TO MAKE SOON IS...

- IF I GET DISCOURAGED, I FEEL BETTER WHEN...

- I AM BECOMING...

- I AM MOST PRODUCTIVE WHEN...

- WHEN I WAS A KID, I
  IMAGINED THAT I WOULD
  GROW UP TO BE...

125 Which **teacher** has the **most patience?**

126 If you made **a documentary about your school**, what would you call it? What would you want to **feature**? Whom would you **interview**?

127 What's something that **challenged you** today?

128 Do you ever feel like **you're doing your best**, but it's not good enough?

129 What did you **do well** today?

130 Would your classes be more interesting if you met more **people** who actually used your **school subjects** in **day-to-day life**?

131 Did anything or anyone **hurt your feelings** today?

132 What **food cheers you up** at lunch?

133 Have you ever had a **hard time admitting** you made **a mistake**?

 134 What makes you **empathize** with a person?

 135 What **vocabulary word** have you learned most recently?

 136 How **quickly** could you learn a **foreign language**?

LEAD by EXAMPLE

- MY FAVORITE MONTH IS...

- MY FAVORITE SEASON IS...

- MY FAVORITE YEAR OF MY LIFE, SO FAR, IS...

- MY FAVORITE HOLIDAY IS...

- THE LONGEST ROAD TRIP I'VE EVER BEEN
  ON WAS...

- WHEN I WAS A KID, THESE WERE THE GAMES
  I LIKED TO PLAY IN THE CAR...

- MY FAVORITE STATE PARK
  OR FIELD TRIP WAS...

137 What kind of **paintings** do you like?

138 What's one thing your school **does really well?**

139 Do you ever feel **exhausted?** What's the **longest** stretch of time that you've felt this way?

140 If your school had one week to **break a world record,** what record would you want to break?

141 What **song** is everyone **obsessed** with right now?

 142 If you were stranded on a **deserted island** and could bring only **one textbook**, which book would you choose?

 143 Have you ever noticed **a rumor** spreading throughout your school?

 144 What **grades** would you give each of your **teachers**?

145 Who is **the tallest person** in your school?

146 Does anyone seem **different** from the person **they were** last year?

147 Are there kids who always try to **break** the rules?

148 If your school gave you more of a say in **what and how you are taught**, what would you change?

LEAD by EXAMPLE

- ONE THING THAT MAKES ME HAPPY IS...

- SOMETHING I HAVE LEARNED ABOUT HAPPINESS IS...

- A PERSON I KNOW WHO ALWAYS SEEMS HAPPY IS...

- ONE THING THAT MAKES ME SAD IS...

- ONE THING I DO WHEN I FEEL SAD IS...

- ONE THING I DO WHEN I NOTICE SOMEONE ELSE IS SAD IS...

149 What's **the best thing that could happen** during a random school day?

150 Is there anyone in your class who always seems **really happy**?

151 Is there anyone who **seems really sad**?

152 Do your **emotions** ever have an impact on **how you behave**?

153 Have you ever been **blamed for something you didn't do?**

 154 Is there **someone you trust** at school?

 155 If you could **vote to change** one thing about your school, what would you vote for? What would **other kids** vote for?

156 If you had to come up with **one question** that **only I** would know the answer to, what would it be?

157 Are there students who are always **really quiet**?

158 What's **the most exciting thing** that happened today?

159 Do you ever have **a hard time** trying your best?

160 If your school had **one room** that possessed **magical powers**, where would it be located? **What kind** of magical powers would it have? **Who** would know about it?

LEAD by EXAMPLE

- SOMETHING THAT HAS BEEN ON MY TO-DO LIST FOR A LONG TIME IS...

- ONE OF MY FAVORITE MOTIVATIONAL QUOTES IS...

- THE MOST INSPIRING PERSON I HAVE EVER MET IS...

- IF I COULD MEET ONE OF MY PERSONAL HEROES, I WOULD CHOOSE...

161 Who was in a **bad mood** today?

162 Have you ever **forgotten someone's name** right after you heard it?

163 Did you have a hard time **motivating yourself** to do something today? What was it?

164 Can you think of a **situation** where you **motivated yourself**? What did you do?

165 When were you the most **bored** you've ever been in **class**?

166 **If you started a company,** which students or teachers at your school would you want to **work** for you?

167 What's your **favorite candy**?

168 What's something you **think** about that adults **never talk about**?

169 Do you prefer to be in the company of **other people** or **by yourself**?

170 Is it important to have **alone time?**

171 Whom does everyone **respect?**

172 Should schools teach **how to have a healthy argument** or conflict?

LEAD by EXAMPLE

- LATELY, I HAVE BEEN STRESSED OUT BY...

- ONE WAY I DEAL WITH STRESSFUL FEELINGS IS...

- TO TRY TO AVOID STRESS I USUALLY...

- I THINK IT'S REALLY BRAVE THAT...

- ONE TIME I ALMOST GAVE UP WAS...

- IF I'M FEELING DOWN, I TRY TO CHEER
  MYSELF UP BY...

173 What do you think life was like **before** people had **refrigerators?**

174 Which classroom has the most interesting **stuff on the walls?**

175 Do you have a **favorite tree?**

176 Do you think your environment at school is one of **healthy stress** or **unhealthy stress?**

177 Are kids **smarter** today than they were **a hundred years ago?**

 178 **Where do you sit** in class?

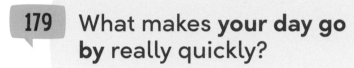 **179** What makes **your day go by** really quickly?

 180 If your history class **had a pet**, what would its **name** be?

181 If you could **study abroad** anywhere in the **world**, where would you go?

182 Do you ever **drift off** when someone else is **talking**?

183 What is one thing you **succeeded** at today? What is one thing you **failed** at?

184 What kind of **future** do you want to **create** for yourself?

LEAD by EXAMPLE

- WHEN I WAS A KID, MY FAVORITE HAT WAS...

- MY FAVORITE SHOES WERE...

- MY FAVORITE ACCESSORY WAS...

- I PLAYED DRESS-UP WITH...

- MY FAMILY MEMBERS WORE...

- ONE SHIRT I WISH I STILL HAD IS...

- ONE OUTFIT I LOVED THAT'S NO LONGER
  IN STYLE WAS...

- A STYLE KIDS ARE WEARING NOW THAT I LIKE IS...

185 What's something at your school that **never seems to be working?**

186 How would a **friend** describe your personality?

187 What **life skills** should be taught in school?

188 What is your **favorite outfit?**

189 Is there **anyone** at school you wish you could **spend more time** with?

 190 What's one thing **you've been meaning to do** that you haven't gotten around to?

 191 Do you like classes **where you have to think** to figure out the answers or classes where you have to **memorize the answers?**

 192 What's the **weirdest word** you've learned?

193 Can any of the **students** at your school **speak another language**?

194 Should **adults** have to go **back to school** to relearn all the things they forgot?

195 Have you had more **good days** or **bad days** this month?

196 Are you ever really **hard on yourself**, even if it's just **internally**?

LEAD by EXAMPLE

- THE BIGGEST HOUSE I HAVE EVER BEEN IN WAS...

- WHEN I GREW UP, THE HOUSE I LIVED IN WAS...

- GROWING UP, I WONDERED WHAT IT WOULD BE LIKE IF I LIVED IN...

- THE FARTHEST I'VE EVER WALKED IS...

- MY FAVORITE BUILDING IS...

- ONE LITTLE SUPERSTITION I HAVE IS...

197 Do you think **other kids struggle** with some of the same things you do **mentally, physically,** or **emotionally?**

---

 198 How many **books** are in your school?

---

 199 Do the **seats at school** help students to have correct **posture?**

---

200 Would you travel to **outer space** if it meant you had to live on a **tiny ship** for a year?

201 What is the **most rewarding job** in the **world**?

202 What is a **sport** that is not part of most schools' **athletic programs** but should be?

203 What's something **romantic** someone has done at school?

204 What **challenges** do you **enjoy** taking on? What challenges do you **dread** facing?

205 If your school **suddenly got $100,000**, what would they use it for?

206 What would you do if you suddenly became **invisible** during school?

207 What makes you **feel loved**?

208 Is there anything you need **my help** or **support** with?

LEAD by EXAMPLE

- FOR BREAKFAST TODAY, I ATE...

- FOR LUNCH TODAY, I ATE...

- MY FAVORITE MIDDAY SNACK IS...

- HERE IS WHAT MAKES ME FEEL GREAT
  AFTER LUNCH...

- I EAT LUNCH IN DIFFERENT PLACES SOMETIMES.
  TODAY, THAT PLACE WAS...

- SOMETIMES I GET MYSELF
  A TREAT DURING THE DAY,
  SUCH AS...

209 What **TV shows** are all the students **talking** about right now?

---

210 How would **a stranger describe your personality** after meeting you for **five minutes**? What about after **five months**?

---

211 Have you noticed whether **certain foods** affect your **mood**?

---

212 Do you notice what affects your **energy level**?

213 What kind of **books** do your teachers have on their **desks** or on their **bookshelves**?

 214 Are the **computers** at your school **fast** or **slow**?

215 What was the **most frustrating thing** that happened today?

216 Does this year seem **harder than last year**?

217 If you taught a class, what **subject** would you **teach**?

218 Which **day** of the school week are people **most engaged**?

219 **If you could go back in time** to the beginning of this week, what would you **tell yourself**? What about the beginning of the **month**? The school **year**?

220 Which of your classmates comes from the **biggest family**?

LEAD by EXAMPLE

- ONE DREAM I STILL REMEMBER IS...

- RECENTLY, MY DREAMS HAVE BEEN...

- I THINK THAT DREAMS TELL YOU...

- WHEN I GO TO SLEEP AT NIGHT, I LIKE TO THINK ABOUT...

- I SLEEP REALLY WELL WHEN...

- WHEN I WAKE UP IN THE MORNING, I...

221 What is the **earliest** you've ever had to **wake up**?

222 What helps you **rest** when your mind is **exhausted**?

223 Which **teacher** has the **worst handwriting**? Which **student** has the worst handwriting?

224 Do you ever **dream** about **school**?

225 Has there ever been a time when you wished someone would have **stuck up for you**?

 226 How could your **school** be better at **recycling**?

 227 What was the **most impactful moment** in **human history**?

 228 If you had to **name the hallways of your school**, what names would you choose?

229 Are some people more **naturally gifted** at certain subjects?

230 Have any of your **teachers** ever been **wrong** about anything?

231 Was anyone having a **bad day** today?

232 What is one thing that you find **distracting** at school?

LEAD by EXAMPLE

- AS AN ADULT, THE LONGEST I'VE GONE WITHOUT SPENDING MONEY WAS...

- ONE THING I HAVE LEARNED ABOUT MONEY IS...

- THE BEST PURCHASE I EVER MADE WAS...

- WHEN I WAS A KID, I WANTED TO SAVE UP MY MONEY FOR...

233 What is the **best way** to **learn something**? Have you experimented with different **learning styles**?

---

234 Who **arrives** at the school **first** in the morning?

---

235 Have you noticed any **strange coincidences** recently?

---

236 Do you think your school has a lot of **money** or has to be **careful** with its **budget**?

237 What is your favorite **dessert**?

238 What **book** would be most useful to have if you were lost in the **wilderness**? What **tool** would be most useful to have?

239 What **country** or **culture** do you want to learn more about?

240 Do any of your **teachers** have a **quote or saying** that they use all the time?

241 Do any of your classmates have **pets**?

242 What **brightens up your day** at school?

243 How often **do you feel sad** at school?

244 How many **beach balls** do you think you could fit into your school?

LEAD by EXAMPLE

- ONE TIME I SHOULD HAVE SAID SORRY WAS...

- ONE LIE THAT I REGRET TELLING IS...

- WHEN I WAS YOUNG, I GOT IN TROUBLE FOR...

- THE BEST APOLOGY THAT I EVER RECEIVED WAS...

245 Is there anyone who seems to **worry too much** about schoolwork?

246 Who seems like they need **more sleep**?

247 Did you **apologize** to anyone today?

248 Have you ever felt like you **shouldn't** have had to **apologize for something**?

249 Do you have someone your age that **you can talk to about anything**? What about a **grown-up**?

 250 Do you ever feel **hopeless**?

 251 Is there anyone who already knows **what they want to do** with their **life**?

252 What's something you have **learned** that **most adults** don't know?

253 If your **teachers** were in a band, what would the **band's name** be?

 254 What would you do if you woke up **tomorrow morning** and it was **today** again?

255 What's one **recipe** you wish you knew **how to make**?

 256 Do you have any **hopes** or **dreams** that **you just can't shake**?

LEAD by EXAMPLE

- SOMETHING I AM REALLY SELF-CONSCIOUS ABOUT IS...

- THE BEST SPEECH I EVER HEARD WAS...

- IF I HAVE TO SPEAK IN FRONT OF PEOPLE, I PREPARE BY...

- THE LARGEST GROUP OF PEOPLE I HAVE EVER SPOKEN TO IS...

- THE MOST NERVOUS I HAVE EVER BEEN WAS...

- TRICKS I USE TO CALM MYSELF DOWN ARE...

257 Would you go to school **six days a week** if it gave you a **longer summer break**?

258 What **games** do the other **kids** at your school like to **play**?

259 What **classes** won't be **necessary** to teach in the **future**?

260 Before you speak up in class, do you **rehearse** what you are going to **say**?

261 If you could go on a **field trip anywhere in the world,** where would you go?

 262 What do you think **your school** spends the **most money** on?

263 Who is the **best** at saying **"please"** and **"thank you"?**

264 Who is the best at **sharing?**

265 Have you ever felt like **people think** you are **weird**? Do you think **other kids** feel that way sometimes? What about **grown-ups**?

 266 When was the last time **someone gave you a compliment**? What was it?

 267 What was one point today when **life was good**?

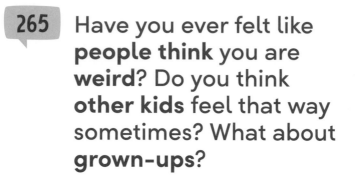 **268** Which **student** never wants any **help**?

LEAD by EXAMPLE

- ONE THING I HAVE LEARNED ABOUT FRIENDSHIP IS...

- WHEN I WAS YOUR AGE, MY BEST FRIEND WAS...

- ONE TIME I FELT LIKE I DIDN'T HAVE MANY FRIENDS WAS...

- ONE PERSON I WISH I COULD SEE MORE OFTEN IS...

- SOMEONE I LOST TOUCH WITH AND WOULD LIKE TO RECONNECT WITH IS...

- WHEN I WANT TO FEEL CONNECTED TO OTHER PEOPLE, I USUALLY...

269 Is there anyone who seems really **responsible** for their **age**?

270 Do you think school is **harder** or **easier** than it was **hundreds of years ago**?

271 Do you **wish** you had **more friends**?

272 Is there **someone** you are thinking of **befriending**?

273 What do you think is the **best job** for someone **your age**?

 274 Is there a **class** that you just **don't enjoy**?

 **275** Have you ever **pretended not to know** something that you actually did know?

 276 Have you **pretended to know** something you didn't know?

277 Would you **learn more or less** if your school had **couches** instead of **chairs?**

 278 Who has an **odd talent?**

 279 Is there anyone who is **really competitive** in your class?

280 Do you prefer learning about **ancient history** or would you rather study **modern history?**

LEAD by EXAMPLE

- MY FAVORITE BOOK THAT I HAD TO READ FOR SCHOOL WAS...

- MY FAVORITE TEACHER WAS...

- MY FAVORITE SUBJECT WAS...

- A SUBJECT I WISH I HAD LEARNED MORE ABOUT WAS...

- I ONCE DID A RESEARCH PROJECT ON...

- MY BEST MEMORY OF SCHOOL IS...

- MY WORST MEMORY OF SCHOOL IS...

281 **How long** would it take you **to write a book?**

---

282 Who at your school has the **most school spirit?**

---

283 If you could time-travel, what would you say to an **earlier version of yourself?**

---

284 If a **future version** of you **time-traveled** back to this moment, what do you think Future You would have to say?

285 Would students be more **interested** if they got to **choose** what **books to read** for a class?

 286 Who is the **kindest student** at school?

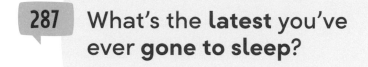

 287 What's the **latest** you've ever **gone to sleep**?

288 If you had to design the **perfect school bus**, what would it be like?

289 Do you ever feel **peer pressure?**

290 Was there ever anything that turned out not to be **as hard as you thought** it would be?

291 Are any of the **teachers** really **bad with technology?**

292 If your school offered a **class** in the middle of the night where you could study **stars and planets** through giant **telescopes,** would you sign up?

LEAD by EXAMPLE

- ONE THING I AM AFRAID OF IS...

- ONE THING I USED TO BE AFRAID OF IS...

- I OVERCAME MY FEAR BECAUSE...

293 What do you **admire about yourself?**

294 What's one thing **other people admire** about you?

295 Is there anyone who really **struggles with math?**

296 Do you ever think about **life and death?**

297 What kind of **tables** are in the **lunchroom** at your school?

 298 If you taught **history**, what could you do to make it really **exciting**?

 299 Did anyone have an **argument** today?

 300 Do you ever feel **disconnected** from **other people**?

301 If you had to bring an **afternoon snack** for the **whole school**, what would you bring?

302 Is there a student that you know has a **good heart** but **doesn't show it**?

303 Are there any **words** that you have only said out loud **one time in your life**?

304 What **drains you** of energy?

LEAD by EXAMPLE

- WHEN I WAS YOUR AGE, MY FAVORITE MOVIE WAS...

- MY FIRST ALBUM (CD, TAPE) WAS...

- MY FIRST CONCERT WAS...

- MY FAVORITE BOOK WAS...

- THE LAST MOVIE I WATCHED WAS...

- A VIDEO I ENJOYED WATCHING WAS...

- THE LAST ACTIVITY I ENJOYED WAS...

305 Do you believe that **people** are **generally good**?

306 Have you ever felt like you knew the **answer** to a question that a teacher asked but **were afraid to say it**?

307 What would a **class about happiness** be like?

308 If you had to **describe your teachers** using the name of a **TV show** or **movie**, what would you choose?

309 Would your **classes** be better if there were **fewer students?**

310 Do you have a **favorite pen or pencil?**

311 If you could **paint** your school **any color**, what color would it be?

312 Who is the **most active** student?

313 What was your **favorite thing** that happened today?

314 If you could **create anything** you wanted in **art class**, with unlimited time and resources, what would you make?

315 Do you like the **layout** of your **school**?

316 If you had to take a **knitting class**, what would you knit?

LEAD by EXAMPLE

- I HAVE SELF-WORTH BECAUSE...

- ONE THING I FAILED AT WHEN I WAS YOUNGER WAS...

- ONE THING I NEVER GAVE UP ON WAS...

- MY BEST MEMORY AS AN ADULT IS...

- ONE OF MY OLDEST MEMORIES IS...

317 Who loves to **learn new things?**

318 Do you think **one person** can **change the world?**

319 Do you ever feel **lonely** or **empty?**

320 Do you **believe in yourself?**

321 Is there anyone who is always **mean**?

322 What's **something interesting** you heard today?

323 Do you have a **favorite drinking fountain**?

324 What could your school do to promote a **healthier lifestyle**?

325 Do your **teachers** explain why you should learn the **subjects** they teach?

326 Do you think the **world outside** your school is generally **fair** or **unfair**?

327 Has anything **happened** in your **classroom** that you thought was **unfair**?

328 Do you think your **teachers** are **fair**?

LEAD by EXAMPLE

- THE MOST I'VE EVER LAUGHED WAS...

- THE LAST TIME I CRIED WAS...

- ONE TIME MY FACE HURT FROM SMILING WAS...

329 Is there **anything coming up** that you are **dreading**?

330 Is there anything coming up that you're **excited** about?

331 Do you **work better** when you have a **deadline** or when you have **unlimited time**?

332 Is there **anyone** who can always **make you laugh**?

333 Is there **anyone** at school who makes you feel **envious**?

334 If you could call **anyone** in the world to **ask about their day,** whom would you call?

335 What makes you **sad**?

336 What **emotional strength** have you had at school this week?

337 Who is the **least organized teacher**?

---

338 What is the **longest book** you have read?

---

339 If you could travel to **any historical site**, where would you go?

---

340 If you had to **design** a **school uniform**, what would it look like?

LEAD by EXAMPLE

- ONE THING I MISS ABOUT BEING A KID IS...

- WHEN YOUR GRANDPARENTS' GENERATION WAS YOUNG, THEY...

- WHEN I WAS A KID, THE MOST POPULAR ACTIVITIES AT RECESS WERE...

- AT MY SCHOOL, LUNCH WAS USUALLY...

341 Do you think you are **kind to others?**

 342 Have you ever noticed someone **taking advantage** of your **kindness** or **generosity?**

 343 Would you rather have a **school-wide game** of **tag** or **hide-and-seek?**

344 What would **college** and **adult recess** be like?

345 In which **class** do you **look at the clock** the most?

346 What is the **hardest job** in the **world**?

347 Does your **school** have a **distinctive smell**?

348 If you could be **pen pals** with a student from anywhere in the world, what **city** or **country** would you pick?

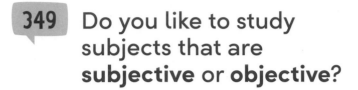 **349** Do you like to study subjects that are **subjective** or **objective**?

 350 Is it okay to **question everything**?

 **351** Which **students** are really **outgoing**?

 **352** Is there **anyone** who always seems **optimistic**?

LEAD by EXAMPLE

- THE BEST DINNER I EVER HAD WAS...

- WHEN I WAS A KID, I LOVED TO EAT...

- WHEN I WAS A KID, I HATED EATING...

- ONE FOOD WE'D ALWAYS HAVE ON HOLIDAYS WAS...

- THE WEIRDEST FOOD I'VE EVER TRIED IS...

- A FOOD I DIDN'T LIKE AS A KID THAT I LOVE TO EAT NOW IS...

- GROWING UP, I ATE A LOT OF...

353 Should **students** still learn how to **farm** and **grow crops**?

---

354 What's one **food** you've always been **afraid to try**?

---

355 What's one food you've always **wanted to try**?

---

356 Can you think of a food that **you didn't think you would like**, but when you tried it, you loved it?

357 Do you prefer to read **old works of fiction** or **newer ones?**

358 Are there certain **walls** or **doors** that you **touch** every time you **walk past** them?

359 What do your **teachers** get really **excited** about?

360 What is the **most popular donut flavor?**

361 What is your **favorite instrument** to hear?

 362 Did you receive any **criticism** today?

 **363** What's the most **memorable conversation** you've had at school?

 364 Is there anyone at school who has really **low self-esteem?**

LEAD by EXAMPLE

- WHEN I WAS A KID, I LIKED TO PLAY...

- LAST TIME I CLIMBED A TREE WAS...

- LAST TIME I RAN THROUGH A SPRINKLER WAS...

- A HOBBY I WISH I DID MORE OFTEN IS...

- MY FAVORITE BOARD GAME IS...

- MY FAVORITE OUTDOOR GAME IS...

- ONE HOBBY THAT I PLAN TO TAKE UP IS...

- ONE THING I WOULD LOVE TO DO BUT AM NOT VERY GOOD AT IS...

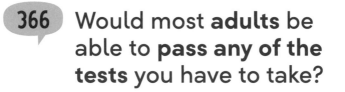 **365** What's the most **comfortable seat** in all of your **classrooms?**

 366 Would most **adults** be able to **pass any of the tests** you have to take?

 367 Would you rather go to school in a **castle** or on a **giant ship?**

368 Who has the **most unique hobby?**

369 If you could build a tiny model of **any building, structure,** or **landscape** in the world, what would you create?

370 What is your favorite **mode of transportation?**

371 What do you think the **very first school** was like?

372 Is there **anyone at school** who always seems to be **sick?**

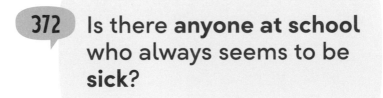

373 Which **teacher** has the **most interesting life story**?

374 Which **teacher** has the hardest time **enforcing the rules?**

375 In what ways could your **school** be **less wasteful?**

376 What makes **time go by** really **quickly?**

LEAD by EXAMPLE

- I FEEL CONFIDENT WHEN...

- I FEEL PROUD WHEN...

- I FEEL ACCEPTED WHEN...

- I FEEL LOVED WHEN...

377 Do you ever have days when **you like the way you look,** and days **when you don't?**

 378 Is there anything you've been **afraid** to **talk to me** about?

 379 Do you know that **you can always come to me** if you are feeling hopeless, no matter what?

380 Is there **anything you wish we talked about** more?

381 If you could skip school and **go anywhere for a day,** where would you want to go?

 382 What would a **class** about **mental health** be like?

 383 How can you tell if someone is in **trouble**?

 384 Can you tell me about a **decision** you had to make **recently**?

385 Is it easier for you to **make decisions right away** or to **wait**?

 386 Would you rather **your life's work** showed up in the future in a **history textbook** or an **art museum**?

 387 If you could **bring a pet to school**, what would you bring?

388 What **class** does everyone **pay attention** in?

LEAD by EXAMPLE

- WHEN I WAS A KID, MY BEDROOM LOOKED LIKE...

- ONE OF MY PRIZED POSSESSIONS WAS...

- AS A KID, I CLEANED MY ROOM ONCE
  A (DAY, WEEK, MONTH)...

389 What is the **oldest book** you have read?

390 If your class could **conduct any science experiment**—with unlimited funds and no injuries—what experiment would you choose?

391 What **pizza topping** have you never tried?

392 What is the **best present** you've ever received?

393 Would you rather take a **creative writing class** or a **journalism class**?

 394 Have you ever had a **great idea** for an **invention**?

 395 Would it be difficult for you to **speak** in front of a group or **teach** a class for **an entire day**?

396 Do you feel **confident** today?

397 Who at school **talks about themselves** a lot?

398 Has anyone you know been to **another country**?

399 What makes you feel **social anxiety**?

400 What **language** do you wish you knew how to **speak**?

LEAD by EXAMPLE

- FIVE YEARS AGO, I WAS PROBABLY...

- ONE YEAR AGO, I WAS PROBABLY...

- ONE MONTH AGO, I WAS PROBABLY...

- ONE WEEK AGO, I WAS PROBABLY...

401 Do you have any **teachers** that always seem to be in a **good mood**?

402 What's the **strangest book** you have read?

403 Who asks the **most questions** in class?

404 What would your **classes** have been like **one hundred years ago**?

405 What **club** or **team** do you wish your school had?

406 If you could change your **school mascot** to anything, what would it be?

407 If your school had a **zoo** with animals that the students cared for, what **animals** would you choose to have?

408 Do you feel that you are able to **set strong boundaries**?

409 Who has the **longest hair in school?**

410 What is **one mistake** that you made today?

411 What do you do **when you make a mistake?**

412 Would you rather go to school for a day on a **train** or on a **ferry boat?**

LEAD by EXAMPLE

- FOR ME, THE MOST PEACEFUL PLACE TO WORK IS...

- WHEN I WAS IN SCHOOL, MY FAVORITE PLACE TO BE WAS...

- AS A KID, I WISHED I COULD SPEND MORE TIME AT...

- THE HARDEST I HAVE EVER WORKED WAS...

- A PROJECT I'M REALLY PROUD OF IS...

- A FUTURE PROJECT I'D LIKE TO TACKLE IS...

413 Do you think schools should teach more about **food** and **eating**?

414 Would you rather **try something new** that you might not be good at or **keep doing what you have already learned** to do well?

415 If your **school** got to create a **national holiday**, what would it be?

416 What's your **favorite classroom**?

417 What are all the students **obsessed with** right now?

418 Does **anyone in your class** seem like a **picky eater**?

419 Does anyone eat the **same food** every day?

420 What do your **teachers** do when they **aren't in school**?

421 Are you ever **afraid of rejection?**

---

422 Does your school do a good job teaching **social skills** and **interaction?**

---

423 If someone painted a **portrait of you,** what would you want to be **wearing?**

---

424 What's one **drink** you've always wanted to **try?**

LEAD by EXAMPLE

- ONE THING I AM AT PEACE WITH IS...

- ONE THING THAT BOTHERS ME IS...

- I AM GOING TO CHOOSE TO BE HAPPY ABOUT...

425 If your school got to pick a **restaurant or chef** to make lunch for the students, whom would everyone **vote** for?

426 Who in your school said the **most words** today?

427 Did anyone have a **birthday** today?

428 Did anything **bring you joy** today?

429 If the students got to choose a **positive slogan** for the school, what would it be?

430 Are there any **students** who **don't seem to get a subject**?

431 Do you think you ever **crossed paths** with any of your **friends** before you officially met them?

432 Should schools teach **psychology**?

433 If you **wrote a book,** what would it be about?

434 Has anyone ever thought you were **doing something wrong** when you weren't?

435 Did you see anyone **show empathy** today?

436 If you got to write the **lead story** for the school **newspaper,** what would you write about?

437 Do you ever have **racing thoughts**?

438 How long would it take you to **run** all the way **around the outside** of your school?

439 What do you think the teachers **talk** about in the **teachers' lounge**?

440 What do you think is **important to learn** in school?

441 If you could throw a **party** that is historically themed, what **era, decade,** or **historical moment** would you choose?

442 What's the **happiest day** you've had at school **this year**?

 443 Would you like to hear about **my day**?

LEAD by EXAMPLE

On the day you
were born,
I remember...

444 Do you know that
I love you?

LEAD by EXAMPLE

On the day you
were born,
I remember...

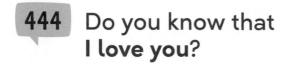

444 Do you know that
I love you?

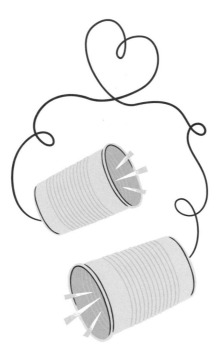